I0117502

Benjamin Franklin DeCosta

A Relation of a Voyage to Sagadahoc

Now First Printed from the Original Manuscript

Benjamin Franklin DeCosta

A Relation of a Voyage to Sagadahoc
Now First Printed from the Original Manuscript

ISBN/EAN: 9783744778909

Printed in Europe, USA, Canada, Australia, Japan

Cover: Foto ©Thomas Meinert / pixelio.de

More available books at **www.hansebooks.com**

A RELATION

OF

A VOYAGE TO SAGADAHOC

NOW FIRST PRINTED FROM THE

Original Manuscript in the Lambeth Palace Library

EDITED WITH PREFACE NOTES AND APPENDIX

BY THE

REV. B. F. DECOSTA

CAMBRIDGE
JOHN WILSON AND SON
University Press
1880

1 - 125

NOTE.

The following journal of a voyage to Sagadahoc was communicated to the Massachusetts Historical Society, and appears in their Proceedings for May, 1880.

The editor is very greatly indebted to Mr. Charles Deane, the Corresponding Secretary of the Society, through whom it was communicated, for his careful supervision of the work as it went through the press.

A small edition has been printed apart from the Proceedings, for private distribution.

B. F. D.

New York, August, 1880.

THE RELATION

OF A VOYAGE UNTO NEW ENGLAND

BEGAN FROM THE LIZARD Y^E FIRST OF
JUNE 1607.

BY CAPT^N POPHAM IN Y^E SHIP Y^E GIFT

[AND]

CAPT^N GILBERT IN Y^E MARY AND JOHN:

WRITTEN BY   .   .   .   .   .   .

& FOUND AMONG Y^E PAPERS OF Y^E TRULY WOR^{SPFUL}

S^R FERDINANDO GORGES K^{NT}

BY ME

WILLIAM GRIFFITH.

[This is not the title given by the author, but was prefixed to the manuscript at a later period.]

RELATION

OF A

VOYAGE TO SAGADAHOC.

EDITORIAL PREFACE.

In the year 1849 the Hakluyt Society published Strachey's work entitled "The Historie of Travaile unto Virginia Britannia," edited by R. H. Major, Esq. Chapters VIII., IX., and X. contained an account of the Popham Colony, planted in the year 1607, at the mouth of the Kennebec River. Prior to the appearance of that work, but few of the details respecting the colony were known. In 1852 the portion of Strachey's "Historie" which included the story of the colony was reprinted, with additional notes, in the Collections of the Massachusetts Historical Society (4th ser. vol. i. p. 219). The following year four chapters of the same part of the "Historie" were printed with new notes in the Collections of the Maine Historical Society (vol. iii. p. 286). In 1862 the Maine Society held a celebration on the site of the ancient colony, publishing the proceedings, during the following year, in a "Memorial Volume." Subsequently, certain features of the undertaking were discussed by several writers in the Boston daily press. In 1866 a number of the articles thus given to the public were reprinted, and a bibliography of the subject was added. No essentially new facts, however, were laid before the public.

This manuscript was found by the writer in the summer of 1875, while engaged in a careful search for historical material. It is now given to the public entire for the first time. By a comparison of the narrative with Strachey's, it will be seen that the manuscript, or at least a tolerable copy, must have passed through his hands, forming indeed the principal source of his knowledge respecting the Popham Colony. Portions of the manuscript were copied by him almost verbatim, though other portions were either epitomized or omitted.

Upon the titlepage of the manuscript, subsequently prefixed to it, the author's name is wanting, but we incline to the opinion, upon the evidence given below, that it was written by James Davies, one of the Council of the colony. The account partially covers the voyage of two ships, the "Gift of God" and the "Mary and John," to the Kennebec in 1607, together with a relation of many events which immediately followed. Unfortunately, the closing portion of the manuscript has disappeared. This mutilation must have occurred since Strachey wrote, as a continuation of the narrative is found in that writer's "Historie." Concerning Strachey himself, comparatively little is known, though he was Secretary to the Virginia Colony in 1609–10. Besides his work on the "Laws of Virginia," published at Oxford, in 1612, he wrote the very interesting account, in Purchas, of the shipwreck of Gates at Bermuda, and narrated subsequent events in Virginia. Of his "Historie of Travaile," he left two copies in manuscript, both referred to by Mr. Major, one of which is preserved in the British Museum, and the other in the Bodleian Library at Oxford. The latter copy lacks the intercalated sketches made on the coast of Maine. From the Oxford manuscript we have drawn the portion corresponding with the lost pages of the narrative, which forms the conclusion of Strachey's "Historie," at pp. 176–180 of the printed volume.

This interesting narrative of "A Voyage unto New England" is now preserved among the treasures of Lambeth Palace Library, London, bound up in the middle of a quarto volume of manuscripts that bear no special relation to the subject of the voyage. The manuscript, however, may be traced very easily in the catalogue. It is numbered 806. The writer was very agreeably surprised one day, when, in the course of searching for material, he came upon the narrative. Application was at once made for permission to copy it for publication, the request being very kindly granted by Dr. Tait, the Archbishop of Canterbury, whose authorization is essential before works of this kind can be thus used. A sort of titlepage has been prefixed to the manuscript, in an early hand, by a former possessor, reciting that it was found among the papers of Sir Ferdinando Gorges by one William Griffith. Gorges died in 1647, and we can hardly suppose that his papers would have been subject to overhauling before that event took place.

The manuscript was difficult to decipher, owing to the peculiarity of the chirography, but there is every reason to suppose that the work has been performed faithfully, as it was done by a copyist selected by the obliging Librarian, Mr. S. W. Kershaw.

As to the authorship of the narrative, Strachey, in his "Historie" (p. 165) relates that, on a certain occasion "The pilot, Captain R. Davies, with twelve others, rowed into the bay," &c. In our manuscript, however, which Strachey used, the author at this place says, "Myself was with 12 others," &c. This shows that the name, "Captain R. Davies," was here inserted by Strachey, on his supposition that Robert Davies was the author of the narrative, and was here describing these incidents. Yet Purchas (vol. v. p. 830), who had this manuscript, and quotes briefly from it, as well as from those of other Sagadahoc colonists, places the name of "James Davies" in the margin, as the author of it. Here is apparently conflicting evidence.

Again, the writer of the narrative frequently speaks of himself, as he did in the above instance, in the first person, as "myself," and we might fairly infer that he adhered to this method. Under the date of September 5, in describing another incident, he introduces the names of "Captain Gilbert, James Davies, and Captain Best," which would seem to show that "James Davies," one of the persons named, was not "myself," the author. It should be added, that the writer, while giving their titles to Gilbert and Best, simply gives the name "James Davies" without any title, as one writing his own name might do.

Robert Davies and James Davies are both spoken of by Strachey and by Smith as "Captains," and as members of the colonial Council; and, so far as we know of the relative character and position of the two men, and we know but little, one would be as likely to have written the narrative as the other. If we had full evidence that Robert Davies was the author, we should not be surprised to find no detailed account of the colony by him during the winter, or during the period of his absence from Sagadahoc,—namely, from the 15th of December, when he re-embarked in the "Mary and John," as its commander, for England, till his return in the following spring, with fresh supplies, when all the remaining colonists went back to England. The brief account we have in the concluding part of the narrative, as shown by what Strachey has preserved, might well have been gathered up by Captain Robert Davies on his return to the colony, in 1608, and added to the previous account.

Of course it will be understood that Strachey did not derive from our narrative the statement, on page 178 of his "Historie," that Captain Robert Davies was despatched away to England in the "Mary and John," "soon after their first arrival." The colony arrived in the early part of August, and the "Mary and John" sailed for home December 15 following, more than four months after their arrival, bearing the letter of Captain Popham to the king.

Whoever the author may have been, it would appear, from his own account, at least, that he was a man of some importance; for as the "Mary and John," on the voyage hither, was approaching Gratiosa, he opposed the opinion of the master and his mates, who thought the island was Flores: "Myself withstood them and reproved them." Possibly the "master" of the "Mary and John" on her voyage hither was Robert Davies, whom Strachey calls "the pilot," the commander or captain being Raleigh Gilbert. The opinion of Purchas, that James Davies was the author of our manuscript, is entitled to great weight, and should perhaps control the evidence.

Strachey must have known both these persons, subsequently, in the southern colony of Virginia. One of the vessels which accompanied the fleet hither in 1609, on which voyage Gates and Somers were wrecked at Bermuda, was the "'Virginia,' which was built in the North Colony," in which "Captain Davies" and "Master Davies" were the chief officers. Surely these can be no other than our Sagadahoc acquaintances. Strachey embarked in the "Sea-Adventure," with Gates and Somers. We find "Captain James Davies" mentioned in a letter of Strachey, written from Virginia in the following year, as commander of "Algernoone Fort," upon Point Comfort.*

Concerning the value of the manuscript in Lambeth Palace Library there can be no question; and it shows very distinctly that Strachey had good authority for the principal part of his narrative relating to the Sagadahoc Colony. He used other authorities also, perhaps one or more of those cited by Purchas in his brief abstract before mentioned. Strachey's whole book, "Historie of Travaile," which embraces an account of the Southern Colony as well, is a compilation, though he probably drew somewhat upon his own experience in his narrative of the latter.

Strachey made some blunders in his summary of our manuscript, but his errors were certainly unintentional. He used the work of Davies without credit, as he did the journals of Gosnold, Pring, and Rosier, but this was in accordance with the custom of the time.

This manuscript we now print is also of value, for the reason that it gives new facts of considerable interest, and leads to a better understanding of the enterprise.

In giving this narrative to the press, it has been thought best to modernize the orthography in those instances where it differed from that of our own day, inasmuch as it often represented the spelling of no particular period. Proper names have been allowed to stand as written.

At the beginning of the seventeenth century, voyagers to the New England coast were still indulging in golden dreams, while at the same time searching for a short passage to the Indies in a region where the breadth of an entire continent barred the way. In the order of Providence, however, these shores were destined to become the field of a nobler quest; and, among scenes hitherto frequented only by maritime adventurers, English colonists were destined to find a home, and lay the foundations of a prosperous commonwealth. The attempt to establish the colony at Sagadahoc pointed to this conclusion.

The first known voyage to New England in the seventeenth century was that of Gosnold, who named Cape Cod, and spent some weeks at Cuttyhunk, on the southern coast of Massachusetts.† In 1603 Martin Pring, with two vessels, lay for several weeks in Plymouth Harbor.‡

On Easter Sunday, May 15, 1605, Captain Waymouth sailed from Dartmouth, England, with intentions that have never been sufficiently explained, sighting land in latitude 41° 20′ N. The coast of Cape Cod appearing dangerous, and having a head wind, he did not attempt the southern course. He was also in need of wood and water, and, moreover, being of an irresolute disposition, he concluded to sail with the wind. As the result, on the 18th he found the island now known

---

* Purchas, vol. iv. pp. 1733, 1748; Neill, Virginia Company of London, pp. 30, 37, 49.
† Historical and Genealogical Register, for Jan. 1878, p. 76.
‡ Ibid. p. 79.

as Monhegan, under which he anchored, hoping that it would prove the "most fortunate ever discovered." Afterward he reached a harbor which he called "Pentecost" and explored a great distance the river which, in the opinion of the writer, was that now known as the Kennebec, where he set up a cross and took possession in the name of King James.

The advantages derived from Monhegan certainly proved considerable, but Sir Ferdinando Gorges lays the stress upon another point, and affirms that the savages captured by Waymouth and carried to England, and trained for future service, were the means "under God, of putting on foot and giving life to all our plantations." What he learned from them encouraged him to use his influence with Sir John Popham; and, finally, by their joint efforts, the king was induced to grant two patents, one for the London Company and one for the Plymouth Company; both being under a general governing body composed of thirteen persons, called the "Council of Virginia." The territory of the London Company included the regions between 34° and 41° N., and that of Plymouth 38° and 45° N. They were entitled to coin money, impose taxes and duties, and exercise a general government for twenty-one years.* The value of Waymouth's voyage, therefore, cannot be questioned, and in no inferior sense may he be regarded as one of the founders of New England. It was under this patent that the Popham Colony was undertaken at the mouth of the Kennebec, then known as Sagadahoc.

It is true that the men who undertook the enterprise did not possess the deliberate purpose essential to immediate success. Nevertheless this may be viewed as preparatory to the scheme afterward unfolded on the New England coast. The enterprise was inaugurated in 1606. Some of the notices of this event, however, are contradictory. Strachey says that Sir John Popham "prepared a tall ship well furnished," which set sail from Plymouth under one "Haines, Maister," who took as "Captaine" one "Martin Prin," and that the ship was captured by the Spaniards at the Azores.† But the ship was not captured there, neither was Pring on board. Sir Ferdinando Gorges states that he himself sent out a ship under Captain Challons, with orders to keep to the northward as far as Cape Breton, and then sail southward to Sagadahoc; but that, when the vessel reached the Azores, Challons fell sick, and his subordinates took the responsibility of sailing by the way of the West Indies, where they were captured by the Spaniards and carried to Spain.‡ The account of Stoneman the Pilot indicates that they were carried southward by the *wind*, and so captured and sent to Spain. Stoneman reached England September 18, and reported to Sir Ferdinando.§

---

* Hazard, vol. i. p. 50.
† "Historie of Travaile," p. 162.
‡ "Brief Narration of the Original Undertakings of the Advancement of Plantations," in 3 Mass. Hist. Coll. vol. vi. pp. 51, 52, and "Brief Relation" of President and Council, in 2 Mass. Hist. Coll. vol. ix. p. 3.
§ Stoneman gives a revolting picture of the barbarities of the Spaniards.

But so earnest were the movers in this enterprise, that, before hearing of the fate of Challons another ship was sent out. The " President and Council " say that Thomas Hanam was captain, and " Martine Prine," master. This was Pring who made the voyage of 1603. On reaching the coast of Maine, Pring failed to find Challons, but Gorges says that he made " a perfect discovery of all those rivers and harbors." In fact, it was the most exact exploration that ever came into his hands.* Hanam also wrote a journal, which Purchas used. He says that Hanam, who sailed to Sagadahoc, "relateth of their beasts, dogs like wolves, of colors black, white, red, grisled : red deer, and a beast bigger, called the mus, &c., of their fowls, fishes, trees : of some ore proved to be silver. Bashabes hath many under-Captains called *Sagamos:* their houses built with withs and covered over with mats, six or seven paces long. He expresseth also the names of their twelve moons or months : as January, Mussekeshoó, February, Gignokiakeshos," &c. †

Reaching the year 1607, there are yet some conflicting statements. The memory of Gorges is at fault when he says that "three sail of ships" were employed. The number of "landmen" he puts at one hundred, but in this he does not include Captains Popham and Gilbert, and "divers other gentlemen of note." Smith makes the same statement as to the number of persons. The " Brief Relation " of the President and Council gives the same number of "landmen," but properly mentions only two ships, while Strachey says that there were " one hundred and twenty persons and planters." The author of this journal, our principal guide in the expedition, does not mention the strength of the colonists. There were no women.

Sailing from Plymouth the last day of May, 1607, and from the Lizard, June 1, at six o'clock in the afternoon, at the end of twenty-four days the expedition reached the Azores. Here the principal ship, the " Mary and John," had a narrow escape from the Netherlanders, who seized Captain Gilbert and charged him with being a pirate.

In the mean while Captain Popham, who commanded the fly boat called the " Gift of God," paid no attention to the signals of distress made by Gilbert's crew, and finally sailed away, apparently either ignorant or careless of what was transpiring. After escaping from the Netherlanders, Gilbert also stood to sea, and crossed the ocean alone, sighting the coast of Nova Scotia, July 28. His landfall, however, has been stated incorrectly by every writer who has touched upon the subject. The earliest opinion, encouraged by Smith, placed the landfall at Monhegan, but after the publication of Strachey's work, it was

See Purchas, vol. iv. p. 1832. Also letter of Gorges to Challons. Cal. State Papers, Colo., under March 13, 1607. Folsom gives the wrong date in his Documents relating to Maine (p. 1), where Gorges calls the leader of the voyage " Chalinge," though in the Brief Narration it is " Challoung." Purchas writes, " Challons," and " Chalenge."
* " Brief Narration," chap. v.
† Purchas, vol. v. p. 830.

supposed by some to have been Mount Desert, while the " Cape " which appears so prominently in the narrative was regarded as Small Point. These were little better than guesses.

The approach to the land, and the subsequent movements of the " Mary and John," are described particularly by the author of the narrative we now print, who was on this ship. Gilbert crossed the southern edge of Grand Bank and passed thence to Sable Bank. According to the soundings, he did not run very far south of Sable Island. Next he stood west-north-west, looking for the land two or three days; but having a light breeze he made only thirty-six leagues. July 30 the land was seen to the north-west, distant about ten leagues. Failing to reach the coast before night, he "struck a hull," so that it was not until three o'clock the next afternoon that the ship got in upon anchorage. The island under which Gilbert anchored in the storm-tossed " Mary and John " lay in 44° 20' N. It was " Ironbound," lying in the well-known harbor or river of La Heve. This place was visited in the autumn of the same year by Lescarbot, then on his way home.

The testimony which covers this subject is unanswerable, yet its character has escaped attention. The pilot had a fair opportunity for making his observations, and that fact alone gave a good clew. The name of the port, " Emanuet," indeed afforded no help, but the name of the chief in authority there was " Messamott," a fact stated by Strachey. Who, therefore, was " Messamott "? Lescarbot tells us that he was a travelled Sagamore, known on the continent as the Sagamore of La Heve. He had been the guest of Grandmont in France. The summer before the Popham colonists arrived, he sailed to Saco with Champlain to arrange a peace with his enemies. Lescarbot celebrates his prowess in " The Muses of New France," and in his narrative, probably borrowed from Champdoré.

The highland seen by Gilbert when out at sea was the well-known landfall of La Heve. It was the port made by Champlain in 1604.* The general description of Champlain also agrees with that of our author. Lescarbot speaks of the abundance of gooseberries found later in the season.

The " Mary and John " lay here over Sunday, where divine worship was doubtless celebrated by the chaplain; and at midnight, Gilbert took a fair north-east breeze and ran down the coast south-west. The next day many islands were seen. The wind being light, they delayed to catch fish; hence Cape Sable was not reached until the morning of August 4. The journal describes its well-known white rocks, though the latitude is given as only 43° N. After rounding the cape, they found a "great deep bay," the Bay of Fundy, and sailing thence seven leagues in a westerly direction they made " three Illands," the well-known Seal Islands, almost exactly seven leagues from the cape, with the Horseshoe Ledge nearly a league to the south-west. Gilbert, knowing his ground, sailed confidently for Sagadahoc, until, supposing that he had gone far enough south, he held in north-

* "Œuvres," tome v. p. 50.

erly, expecting to see the high land. On the afternoon of August 5, the Camden Hills appeared, the three double peaks of which rose above the waves, and were sketched by the writer, who thought them ten miles away, but recognized them as the Penobscot Range. He also observes that this is the first land seen after leaving the cape, being thirty-four hours on the way, evidently with little wind.

Standing in toward the west, they next sighted three islands, lying east and west, whose white rocks shone "like unto Dover clifts," the Matinicus group, which, on this course, *appear* as three. Strachey adds, evidently quoting an exact authority, "There lyeth so-west from the easternmost of the three islands a white rocky island." This is Matinicus Rock, which now bears a lighthouse.

Coming nearer the mountains and to the westward of Matinicus, two of the double peaks already seen rose from the waves, each becoming one. Thence the "Mary and John" held westward eight leagues, and sighted three other islands, Monhegan, Metinic, and Burnt Island, the outer of the Georges group. Under Monhegan, an island already visited and named by Champlain "Ship Island" (*La Nef*), Gilbert dropped anchor.

The succeeding movements of the expedition are tolerably plain, but the outward voyage is now interpreted for the first time. The statements of the journal, when understood, agree with the actual courses, and prove that the master, Robert Davies, or whoever he may have been, was a correct and observing navigator. The modern coast pilot is hardly more clear.

Landing upon the Island of Monhegan, named by Waymouth St. George, a cross was found "set up," the author says, as "we suppose" by Waymouth. In this, however, the company were doubtless at fault, yet the supposition has been accepted as a fact, and has led to much confusion in connection with the voyage of Waymouth. It may have been set up by Pring, who, in 1606, made his exploration of Sagadahoc, and probably sailed to Waymouth's landfall; or by Champlain, in the autumn of 1604.

The next morning, to their great joy, they were joined by the "Gift," now seen for the first time since they parted at the Azores. There was no room, however, for recrimination. At midnight, Gilbert left Monhegan, where the two vessels lay at anchor, and with a dozen men, including the Indian "Skidwarres," a name, according to Rosier, signifying a "gentleman," rowed to Pemaquid, moving with measured stroke among the "gallant islands" that flung down their shadows upon the calm tide. Landing, and crossing Pemaquid Point, they reached an Indian village, and met Nahanada a Sagamore, one of the Indians captured by Waymouth, and who had been returned by Pring the previous year. This chief, though at first alarmed, received the English with joy, after which Gilbert returned to his ship. The next day being Sunday, the members of the expedition landed on Monhegan, and, under the shadow of the cross, they observed what may be called the first English Thanksgiving in New England, the preacher being the Rev. Richard Seymour, who conducted services, we may well suppose, according to the Book of Common Prayer.*

Sunday being past, another visit was made to Nahanada, but with no result beyond the desertion of Skidwarres: after which they sailed for Sagadahoc, where the " Mary and John " narrowly escaped being wrecked, — finally getting into harbor on Sunday forenoon, August 16. Then followed a boat expedition up the river. Afterward a site was selected for the fort, and the colony duly organized, the company possessing all the powers of a commonwealth. As the fort progressed, Digby, the shipwright, proceeded to build a pinnace, the " Virginia," a craft that afterward did good service on the ocean. Captain Gilbert also explored the Sheepscot River, and later gained the upper reaches of the Kennebec.

The manuscript ends after alluding to the meeting with Sabenor, " Lord of the river of Sagadehock." Strachey, however, continues the account in language which indicates that he is employing the remainder of our narrative. At the end he adds some items perhaps not found in the authority which he had so liberally used. As already mentioned, he is clearly in error when he says that the " Mary and John " was sent back " soon after their first arrival," as the vessel was detained to receive the letter of President Popham addressed to King James, dated Dec. 13, 1607, sailing two days after.

Strachey relates that after the departure of Davies, they finished the fort and built fifty houses therein, besides a church, evidently a little chapel, and a storehouse. " Fifty," however, is doubtless a clerical error for five, as in one place he puts fourteen leagues for forty. Five houses would have been ample for the little company, and would at the same time fill up all the space inside the fort. The President and Council speak simply of " their lodgings "; while our author, on August 31, mentions only " the storehouse." Nevertheless, the fort, with twelve guns and seven buildings, must have appeared quite imposing.

During the winter they seem to have done some exploration, but the season was one of unusual severity both in Europe and America, and before the cold weather was over Captain Popham died. According to Purchas, this event took place February 5 † The " Brief Relation " says that this was the only man that died there, which, technically, may be true; but the journal of Gilbert shows that " Master Patteson was slain by the Savages of Nanhoc, a River of the Tarentines." According to Gorges, the storehouse, containing the most of their provisions, was burned during the winter; ‡ and Harlow says that the " short commons caused a fear of mutiny." Nevertheless, a considerable quantity of furs rewarded their exertions, and a " good store of sarsaparilla " was gathered. The colonists also finished their pinnace, which afterward sailed between England and Virginia.§

---

* Popham Memorial, p. 101.
† Purchas, vol. v. p. 830.   ‡ Ibid.
§ In 1609 she is mentioned as " a boat built in the north colony." See *ante*, p. 9.

Captain Gilbert, it appears, heard a story reported by David Ingram,[*] in 1569, where he says, "The people told our men of Cannibals, near Sagadahoc, with teeth three inches long," probably deformed Tarrantines. The natives also reported an open sea inland, and the colonists believed that they were not far from China. Popham reported the sea to King James,[†] as Verrazano reported his open sea to Francis I. Gilbert, not to be outdone by the nutmegs which Popham reported, discovered a lake of hot water.[‡] During the winter, religious services were maintained with good results.

Stories, originally put in circulation by the French, represent that eleven of the colonists were murdered by the Indians. Father Biard, however, did not understand the Indian language, yet he says that when he visited Kennebec in 1611, he made inquiries about the English, and was told that they came in 1608, and had a kind leader who died, and that the next year the Indians quarrelled with the English, who attacked them with dogs and fired upon them with cannon. But as the colonists left in 1608, they could not have been guilty of the acts alluded to. The reference to dogs recalls circumstances connected with Waymouth's voyage, while the real offender probably was Henry Hudson, who, in 1609, entered Somes's Sound at Mount Desert, and there, in the most cruel manner, attacked and plundered the savages.[§] After getting all he could of the savages by fair means, Hudson's pilot says: " In the morning we manned our scute with four muskets and six men, and took one of their shallops and brought it aboard. Then we manned our boat and scute with twelve men and muskets and two stone pieces, or murderers, and drove the savages from their houses and took the spoil of them."[‖] It may have been this disgraceful and unprovoked attack by the crew of the " Half Moon," who were part English and part Dutch, that has been attributed to the colonists at Sagadahoc. The Indians who gave the information were not of the local tribe, whose peaceable disposition was vouched for, in 1616, by Brawnde; while it was the Pemaquid chief, Samoset, who hailed the Plymouth Pilgrims with the words, " Welcome, Englishmen." It is hardly to be supposed that the savages around Sagadahoc had ever been fired upon with cannon.

Still, though the relations of the colonists to the Indians were peaceful, their enterprise did not succeed; and when Captain Davies returned in the spring, he found the company greatly discouraged, no mines having been found, which Strachey says was " the main

---

* Hakluyt, London, 1589, pp. 558–561.
† Maine Hist. Coll. vol. v. p. 357.
‡ Purchas, vol. v. p. 830.
§ Biard wrote two versions of this story. "Rélations des Jésuites," tome i. p. 37. Quebec, 1858; and Carayon's " Première Mission," p. 70. See " Sailing Directions of Henry Hudson." In a boastful spirit, the Indians may have changed *one* to *eleven*; but it is more likely that they gave the account to Biard in their bad French, and thus confused *un* with *onze*, as the two words are pronounced so nearly alike.
‖ Juet in Asher's " Henry Hudson," p. 61.

intended benefit expected." The presence of Captain Gilbert was also required in England, and Chief Justice Popham being dead, it was concluded to abandon the settlement. Details of the return voyage are wanting, but the colonists must have gone home in a ship that was well furnished with every thing needed to maintain them in the new world. The pinnace was also used on the return passage.

"This," says Strachey, "was the end of that northern colony upon the River Sachadehoc." No mention is afterward made of any return of the English; and the only recorded visit is that of the French in the autumn of 1611, where no resident was found, the paths leading to the fort being untrodden. Biard says that, in company with Biencourt, he reached the Kennebec from the east, October 28. Entering the harbor where, in 1607, Popham had moored the "Gift" and the "Mary and John," the French were all animation, and at once hastened to view the stronghold built by the English. As they approached the works they knew they were safe, all things indicating the absence of occupants. Biard writes: "Straightway all our people landed, desirous to see the fort of the English, because we had learned from the paths that no person was there. At first they began to praise and extol the enterprise of the English, and to enumerate the advantages of the place"; soon, however, he testifies, they saw the situation with a military eye, and discovered that the ground was badly chosen, as another fort, properly placed, would have cut them off from both the river and the sea.[*]

Such is the only known description of the place written at that period. The French were evidently impressed by the magnitude of the work. It indicated enterprise, and proved that the builders wrought with regard to something more than a transient occupation. Of the dwellings, nevertheless, Biard says nothing.

Smith says with reference to the enterprise, "They all returned for England in the yeere 1608, and thus the plantation was begun and ended in one yeere, and the country esteemed as a cold, barren, mountainous desert." Gorges also says, "They all resolved to quit the place and with one consent to [come] away."[†] The President and Council also say, "The whole company resolve upon nothing but their return with the ships."[‡]

Yet at all events, the English claimed the coast without qualification, and "Sir Francis Popham having the ships and provision which remained of the company, and supplying what was necessary for his purpose, sent divers times to the coast for trade and fishing."[§] In 1611, Harlow confiscated a French ship for intruding upon the waters of Maine. When Biencourt sailed to the site of the colony, it was expressly to attack the English, who were supposed to be there, though such was not the case, as already related. Smith, in 1614,

---

* Carayon, p. 63. See Hist. Mag., Sept., 1866, where the French of the narrative is misunderstood.
† "Brief Narrative," p. 10.   ‡ "Brief Relation," p. 3.
§ "Brief Relation," p. 4.

found one of Francis Popham's ships that had frequented the port opposite Monhegan for " many years," for fishing and trading in furs. Vines wintered in the country once, and others were known to have spent the cold season on Monhegan.

Concerning the character and the merits of the colonists of Sagadahoc, there has been some warm discussion, though no established facts have been produced that reflect upon their reputation. The colonists were probably no better than the average men of their class, yet there is nothing to indicate that there were any among them who required disciplinary treatment. The Lord Chief Justice has been denounced for his severe conduct of the courts of justice and for the sins of his youth ; but impartial critics will allow that this is altogether aside from the question. So far as we actually know, the course pursued by the colonists was humane and pacific. One of their number was killed by the Tarrantines of the east, while the loss of their provisions induced the fear of a mutiny, yet the temptation to indulge in disorder was resisted. Industry and order seemed to have prevailed, and due respect was shown for the services of religion, the bearing of the English worshippers led by Chaplain Seymour being such as to recommend to the simple savage a faith which he could not comprehend. When, however, it was found that the main purpose for which the colony was undertaken could not be achieved, they departed to employ their activities in another sphere.

Among those who have brought charges against the Popham colonists may be mentioned Aubrey, in his " Letters," &c., vol. ii. p. 495 ; and Sir William Alexander, " Map and Description," p. 30. Bacon's Essay on " Plantations " has also been used. We have cited Alexander in the " Appendix." The replies to these attacks are well known, among them being papers by the late Dr. Ballard of Brunswick, Maine.

B. F. DeCosta.

[A VOYAGE TO SAGADAHOC.]

Departed from the Lyzard the first day of June, A.D. [1607], being Monday, about six of the clock in the afternoon, and it bore off me then north-east and by north eight leagues off.

From hence directed our course for the Islands of Flowers and Corve, in the which we were twenty-four days attaining of it, at which time we still kept the sea and never saw but one sail, being a ship of Salcom * bound for the Newfoundland, wherein was one Sosser [?] of Dartmouth, master in her.

The twenty-fifth day of June we fell with the Island of Garsera,† one of the islands of the Azores, and it bore off us then south and by east ten leagues off, our master and his mates making it to be Flowers, but myself withstood them and reproved them in their error, as afterward it appeared manifestly, and then stood round for Flowers. The 26th of June we had sight of Flowers and Corve, and the 27th, in the morning early, we were hard aboard Flowers, and stood in for to find good road for to anchor, whereby to take in wood and water. The 28th we descried two sails standing in for Flowers, whereby we presently weighed anchor, and stood towards the road of Santa Cruz, being near three leagues from the place where we watered. There Captain Popham anchored to take in wood and water, but it was so calm that we could not recover or get unto him before the day came on.

The 29th of June being Monday, early in the morning those two sails we had seen the night before were near unto·us, and being calm they sent their boats, being full of men, towards us, and after the order of the sea they hailed us, demanding us of whence we were, the which we told them and found them to be Flemens and the state's ships. One

---

* Salcombe. — B. F. D.

† The reader will understand that by "Garsera," "Flowers," and "Corve," the islands of Gratiosa, Flores, and Corvo, belonging to the group of the Azores Islands, are intended. — B. F. D.

of our company, named John Govett, of Plymouth, knew the captain of one of the ships, for that he had been at sea with him. Having acquainted Captain Gilbert of this, and being all friends, he desired the captain of the Dutch to come near and take a can of beer, the which he thankfully accepted, we still keeping ourselves in a readiness both of our small shot and great. The Dutch captain being come to our ship's side, Captain Gilbert desired him to come aboard him and entertained him in the best sort he could. This done, they to requite his kind entertainment desired him that he would go aboard with them, and upon their earnest entreaty he went with them, taking three or four gentle[men] with them, but when they had him aboard of them they there kept him perforce, charging him that he was a pirate, and still threatening himself and his gentlemen with him to throw them all overboard, and to take our ship from us.* In this sort they kept them from ten of the clock morning until eight of the clock night, using some of his gentlemen in most vile manner, as setting some of them in the bilboes, buffeting of others, and other most vile and shameful abuses; but in the end having seen our commission, the which was proffered unto them at the first, but they refused to see it, and the greatest cause doubting of the Englishmen being of their own company who had promised Captain Gilbert that if they proffered to perform that which they still threatened him that then they all would rise with him, and either end their lives in his defence, or suppress the ship; the which the Dutch perceiving, presently set them at liberty, and sent them aboard unto us again, to our no small joy.† Captain Popham, all this time being in the wind of us, never would come round unto us, notwithstanding we making all the signs that possibly we might, by striking our topsail and hoisting it again three times, and making towards him all that ever we possibly could, so here we lost company of him, being the 29th day of June, about eight of the clock at night, being six leagues from Flowers, west-north-west, we standing our course for Vyrgenia. The 30th we lay in sight of the island.

The first day of July being Wednesday, we departed from the Island of Flowers, being ten leagues south-west from it.

From hence we always kept our course to the westward as much as

---

* Possibly there was some connection between the conduct of the Dutch and the state of feeling indicated by Rosier, where, in the introduction to Waymouth's voyage, he says, "After these purposed designs were concluded, I was animated to publish this brief relation, and not before; because some foreign nation (being fully assured of the fruitfulness of the country) have hoped hereby to gain some knowledge of the place, seeing they could not allure our captain or any special man of our company to combine with them for their direction, nor obtain their purpose in conveying away our savages, which was busily in practice." 3 Mass. Hist. Coll. vol. viii. p. 127. The Dutch certainly made strong efforts to secure New England. — B. F. D.

† Part of this sentence is obscure. We interpret it thus: that the captain of the Dutch ship "doubting," that is, *fearing* that the Englishmen, making part of his own ship's company, might rise, as they had promised or threatened to do, to prevent any additional outrage on Captain Gilbert and his companions, was induced to liberate them. — B. F. D.

wind and weather would permit, until the 27th day of July, during which time we oftentimes sounded, but could never find ground. This 27th, early in the morning, we sounded, and had ground but eighteen fathoms,* being then in the latitude of 43⅔°; here we fished three hours, and took near two hundred of cod, very great and large fish, bigger and larger fish than that which comes from the Bank of the Newfoundland; here we might have laden our ship in less time than a month.

From hence the wind being at south-west, we set our sails and stood by the wind, west north-west towards the land, always sounding for our better knowledge as we ran towards the mainland from the bank.

From this bank we kept our course west north-west thirty-six leagues, which is from the 27th of July until the 30th of July, in which time we ran thirty-six leagues, as is before said, and then we saw the land † about ten of the clock in the morning, bearing north-west from us about ten leagues, and then we sounded and had a hundred fathoms black ooze here. As we came in towards the land from this bank we still found deep water; the deepest within the bank is one hundred and sixty fathoms, and in one hundred fathom ‡ you shall see the land if it be clear weather; after you pass the bank the ground is still black ooze until you come near the shore. This day we stood in for the land, but could not recover it before the night took us, so we stood a little from it and there struck a hull until the next day, being the last of July: here lying at hull we took great store of codfishes, the biggest and largest that I ever saw, or any man in our ship. This day, being the last of July, about three of the clock in the afternoon we recovered the shore and came to an anchor under an island, for all this coast is full of islands or broken land, but very sound and good shipping to go by them, the water deep, eighteen or twenty fathoms hard aboard them.

This island standeth in the latitude of 44¼°.§ and here we had not

---

* There is only one part of the Bank where, according to the "Atlantic Neptune," this depth is found. — B. F. D.

† The land seen was either Cape La Heve or the Aspotogeon Hills, which are close by. The cape is an abrupt cliff a hundred and seven feet high, pushing boldly out to sea, while the hills are very noticeable far away at sea. — B. F. D.

‡ This deep water is found on the charts as indicated by the journal. The deepest inside Sable Bank, shown by the "Atlantic Neptune," is one hundred and fifty-two fathoms, which occurs in the course sailed. About thirty miles south-east of Cape La Heve, a hundred fathoms are found, indicating with tolerable precision the position of the "Mary and John" when land was first seen. — B. F. D.

§ Ironbound Island lies precisely in this latitude at the mouth of the La Heve River. Blunt says, "The shores are bold, and much indented with irregular inlets or bays." In the vicinity, twenty fathoms of water are common. "Coast Pilot," 21st ed. 1867, p. 195. Mr. Major, misled by Captain John Smith, and neglecting the fact that points of eastern Nova Scotia lie in the same latitude as parts of the Maine coast, says, "The latitude here given would lead to the supposition that the island referred to was Mount Desert Island in Frenchman's Bay; but nearly all other histories record Manhegin Island as the point at which they first landed." "Historie of Travaile," pp. 165, 166 n. Following Smith, Mr. Bancroft makes the first landing at Monhegan, vol. i. p. 205, ed. 1876. — B. F. D.

been at an anchor past two hours before we espied a bisken shallop coming towards us, having in her eight savages and a little savage boy. They came near unto us and spoke unto us in their language, and we making signs to them that they should come aboard of us, showing unto them knives, glasses, beads, and throwing into their boat some biscuit, but for all this they would not come aboard of us, but making show to go from us, we suffered them. So when they were a little from us, and seeing we proffered them no wrong, of their own accord returned and came aboard of us, and three of them stayed all that night with us. The rest departed in the shallop to the shore, making signs unto us that they would return unto us again the next day.

The next day the same savages, with three savage women, being the first day of August, returned unto us, bringing with them some few skins of beaver in another bisken shallop, proffering their skins to truck with us.* But they demanded over-much for them, and we seemed to make light of them ; and

So then the other three which had stayed with us all night went into the shallop, and so they departed. It seemeth that the French † hath trade with them, for they use many French words. The chief commander of these parts is called Messamott, ‡ and the river or har-

---

* Lescarbot speaks of his traffic here. Evidently it was a well-known trading post. — B. F. D.

† Savalet of Canso was doubtless among their customers, and furnished them with European shallops. "Nouvelle France," p. 604. — B. F. D.

‡ Champlain spells the name "Messamonët," and mentions his visit to Saco, in company with "Secondon." "Œuvres," tome ii. p. 92. Lescarbot describes his doings there in full : " From this isle they went to the river of Olmechin, a port of Choüakoet, where Marchin and the said Olmechin brought a Souriquois prisoner (and therefore their enemy) to Sieur Poutrincourt, whom they gave him freely. Two hours after there arrived two savages, one an Etechemin named Chkoudun, captain of the River St. John, called by the savages Oigoudi ; the other Souriquois named Messamoet, captain or Sagamore in the river of the port La Heve, where this prisoner was taken. They had a great quantity of mer-chandise trucked with the French, which they came to sell, viz., large, medium, and small kettles, hatchets, knives, gowns, short mantles, red waistcoats, biscuit, and other things. Thereupon there arrived twelve or fifteen boats full of sav-ages of Olmechin's following, in good order, their faces painted according to their custom, in beautifying themselves, having the bow and arrow in hand, and the quiver which they laid down. Then Messamoet commenced his harangue before the savages, 'reminding them that in the past they had often been at amity, and that they might easily overcome their enemies, if they would act understand-ingly and make use of their friendship with the French, who were then present in order to reconnoitre the country, to the end that they might bring them com-modities in the future, and aid them with their strength which he knew,' and he was able to represent to them so much better, because he who spoke had formerly been in France, and dwelt in the house of Grandmont, Governor of Ba-yonne. Finally, his speech continued almost an hour with much vehemence and feeling, and with a gesture of body and arms such as is required in a good orator." "Nouvelle France," p. 559, ed. 1612. All this, however, together with his gifts, failed, and the chief went away resolved upon war, which the Saco tribe had already prosecuted as far as La Heve. See also Lescarbot's reference to the warlike actions of this chief in "Les Muses de la Nouvelle France," p. 46, ed. 1612. He probably went on a visit to France in one of De Mont's ships. — B. F. D.

bor is called Emannett.* We take these people to be the Tarentyns †
[and these people, as we have learned since, do make wars with Sasanoa, the chief commander to the westward, where we have planted,
and this summer they killed his son]. ‡

So the savages departed from us, and came no more unto us. After
they were departed from us we hoisted out our boat, wherein myself §
was with twelve others, and rowed to the shore, and landed on this
island that we rode under, the which we found to be a gallant island,
full of high and mighty trees of sundry sorts ; here we also found
abundance of gooseberries,‖ strawberries, raspberries, and whorts. So
we returned and came aboard.

Sunday being the 2d of August, after dinner our boat went to the
shore again to fill fresh water ; where, after they had filled their water,
there came four savages unto them, having their bows and arrows in
their hands, making show unto them to have them come to the shore.
But our sailors having filled their water would not go to the shore
unto them, but returned and came aboard, being about five of the clock
in the afternoon. So the boat went presently from the ship unto a point
of an island, and there, at low water, in an hour killed near fifty great
lobsters. You shall see them where they lie in shoal water, not past
a yard deep, and with a great hook made fast to a staff, you shall hitch
them up there, a great store of them ; you may near load a ship with
them, and they are of great bigness : I have not seen the like in England. So the boat returned aboard, and we took our boat in ; and
about midnight the wind came fair at nôrth-east. We set sail and
departed from thence, keeping our course south-west, for so the coast
lieth.

Monday being the 3d of August, in the morning we were fair by
the shore, and so sailed along the coast ; we saw many islands all along
the coast, and great sounds going betwixt them, but we could make
proof of none for want of a pinnace ; here we found fish still all along
the coast as we sailed.

Tuesday being the 4th of August, in the morning, five of the clock,
we were athwart of a cape ¶ or headland, lying in the latitude of 43°,

---

* We have not yet found any other reference to the Indian name of the river
La Heve in the early chronicles. — B. F. D.

† On these people see Maine Hist. Soc. Coll. vol vii. p. 95. — B. F. D.

‡ The part enclosed in brackets was, of course, added by the author at a
later period. For the account of the death of Sasanoa, see later, under August
22. — B. F. D.

§ Strachey, who may have known the author of this journal, says that this
person was the pilot, R. Davies. Purchas also used the journal and attributes
it to James Davies (vol. v. p. 830). — B. F. D.

‖ Lescarbot says, "And in the same port we saw the cod bite the hook.
There we found an abundance of red gooseberries (grozelles rouges), and a mar-
cassite of copper mine. There we had some traffic in peltry with the savages."
"Nouvelle France," ed. 1612, p. 604. Purchas, vol. iv. p. 1640. Champlain
puts the Cape of La Heve in 44° 5', and speaks of the islands as covered with
pines, and the mainland with oaks, chestnuts, &c. "Œuvres," tome ii. p. 8. —
B. F. D.

¶ Whether or not our author meant to say that the cape was exactly in latitude 43° N. is not clear. The cape in question was Cape Sable, which is in

and came very near unto it. It is very low land, showing white like sand, but it is white rocks ; and very strong tides * goeth here from the place we stopped at, being in 44½ . Until this cape or headland it is all broken land and full of islands, and large sounds betwixt them, and here we found fish abundance, so large and great as I never saw the like cods before, neither any in our ship.

After we passed this cape or headland, the land falleth away and lyeth in north-west and by north into a great deep bay.† We kept our course from this headland west and west and by south seven leagues, and came to three islands,‡ where coming near unto them we found on the south-east side of them a great ledge of rocks,§ lying near a league into the sea, the which we perceiving tacked our ship, and the wind being large to north-east cleared ourselves of them, keeping still our course to the westward, west and by south, and west south-west until midnight, then after we held in more northerly.

Wednesday being the 5th of August, from after midnight we held in west north-west until three of the clock afternoon of the same, and then we saw the land again, bearing from us north-west and by north, and it riseth in this form hereunder. Ten or twelve leagues from you,

---

43° 25′. If he meant to be exact, he was in error to the extent indicated. Mr. Major took the ground that he was in error "more than half a degree." This was assumed to accommodate his theory that the cape was Cape Small Point. He says, " In order to verify and define in modern nomenclature, the description of the course held by the adventurers . . . a very beautiful and elaborate map of this coast, in the British Museum, on a scale of two miles to an inch, has been used "; and he concludes that while the headland was Small Point, the three islands were the Damiscove, Wood, and Outer Heron Islands, with the Pumpkin Ledges. He says "no more southerly cape" would offer the requisite island ; whereas what he needed was a *northerly* cape. The fact that the " Mary and John " made her first port, coming in immediately from a well-known fishing bank, alone would be sufficient to prove that the landfall was not on the Maine coast. See Major's remarks in " Historic," p. 166 *n*. The cape described as "white like sand" was Cape Sable, so called at an early period by the French on account of the *sablou* or sand. If the cape had been Small Point, and the " Mary and John " had continued on the course described, the colonists would have approached the interior of Maine. — B. F. D.

* Blunt's Coast Pilot describes the strong tides running " at the rate of three and sometimes four knots an hour." — B. F. D.

† Bay of Fundy. This, perhaps, may be regarded as the earliest, or one of the earliest, references to the bay by the English; unless Hakluyt had it in mind when he spoke of the " Bay of Menan." (3 Mass. Hist. Coll vol. viii. p. 107.) On the map of Mollineux (1600) projected by Wright, this bay stands apart from the unnamed gulf which seems to indicate the Bay of Fundy. The Continental maps of the sixteenth century, however, commencing with Verrazano (1529), indicate the bay with distinctness, whether it is called *Terra onde, houdo, condo, fondo, fonda,* or Fundy. See the Verrazano map, in " Verrazano the Explorer," revised from Mag. of American History. Barnes & Co , New York, 1880. — B. F. D.

‡ This group is composed of what is now known as " Seal " and the " Mud Islands." On some charts one name is applied to all. If the smallest were included, they would number four. Sailing to the southward the navigator would notice only three. — B. F. D.

§ This ledge, according to Blunt, " is called the Horseshoe, and runs out two and one-half miles, south-east by south." The description is almost scientifically exact. — B. F. D.

there are three high mountains that lie in upon the mainland near unto the river of Penobscot, in which river the Bashabe * makes his abode, the chief commander of those parts, and stretcheth unto the river of Sagadehock under his command. You shall see these high mountains when you shall not perceive the mainland under it, they are of such an exceeding height: and note that from the cape or headland before spoken of, until these high mountains, we never saw any land except those three islands also before mentioned. We stood in right with these mountains until the next day.†

Thursday being the 6th of August, we stood in with this high land, until twelve o'clock noon, and then I found the ship to be in 43¼°‡ of my observation.§ From thence we set our course and stood away due west, and saw three other islands lying together, being low and flat by the water, showing white as if it were sand, but it is white rocks making show afar off almost like unto Dover cliffs.‖

These three islands lie due east and west one of the other, so we came fair by them, and as we came to the westward the high land before spoken of showed itself in this form as followeth.¶

---

* The article prefixed does not prove that the writer meant to give the word "bashabe" as a title. Afterward he speaks of their Indian guide as "the Skidwarres." See, on this subject, Maine Hist. Soc. Coll. vol. vii. p. 95, and Hist. Mag., April, 1868. Strachey adds that the mainland where the mountains stood was "the land called Segohquet." The distance is exaggerated.— B. F. D.

† These three mounts are the same as those given by Strachey in his "Historie" (p. 167). They represent the Camden and Union mountains. The two double peaks at the left represent the four principal peaks of the Union range, while that on the right represents Megunticook. — B. F. D.

‡ Strachey (p. 167) makes the latitude 43°. — B. F. D.

§ It would appear that our author either understood navigation, or used the reckoning of the pilot. In fact he may have used a large portion of his journal, and modified some of the statements, which would account for the variations of Strachey, supposing the latter to have followed another authority here, in part. — B. F. D.

‖ These were the Matinicus Islands. — B. F. D.

¶ Upon getting nearer, the mountains rose from the sea, and the double peaks were united. By a comparison of this view with the recently published sketch of the Coast Survey, the resemblance may be traced, though this ancient sketch is very rude. In the "Historie" (p. 168), another view is given that our manuscript omits. The Oxford MS. omits all these sketches. Our sketches have no indication of foliage on the hill-tops. — B. F. D.

From hence we kept still our course west and west by north towards three other islands that we saw lying from these islands before spoken of eight leagues, and about ten of the clock at night we recovered them, and having sent in our boat before night to view it, for that it was calm, and to sound it and see what good anchoring was under it, we bore in with one of them, the which as we came in by we still sounded, and found very deep water forty fathom hard aboard of it. So we stood in into a cove * in it, and had twelve fathom water, and there we anchored until the morning, and when the day appeared we saw we were environed round about with islands; you might have told near thirty islands round about us from aboard our ship.†

This island we call St. Georges Island, for that we here found a cross set up, the which we suppose was set up by George Wayman.‡

Friday being the 7th of August we weighed our anchor, whereby to bring our ship in more better safety howsoever the wind should happen to blow, and about ten of the clock in the morning, as we were standing off a little from the island, we descried a sail standing in towards this island, and we presently made towards her and found it to be the "Gyfte," our consort; so being all joyful of our happy meeting, we both stood in again for the island we rode under before, and there we anchored both together.§

This night following, about midnight, Captain Gilbert caused his ship's boat to be manned and took to himself thirteen other, myself being one, being fourteen persons in all, and took the Indian Skidwarres with us. The weather being fair and the wind calm, we rowed to the west in amongst many gallant islands, and found the river of Pemaquyd to be but four leagues west from the island we call St. Georges, where our ship remained still at anchor.

Here we landed in a little cove ‖ by Skidwarres' direction, and

---

* This cove does not appear to have been the harbor formed by Mananas which lies close to Monhegan, but a sheltered spot north of the harbor.— B. F. D.

† The islands are certainly numerous.— B. F. D.

‡ There is no proof that the supposition was correct.— B. F. D.

§ First meeting of the ships. Popham appeared to know the anchorage better than Gilbert.— B. F. D.

‖ It would appear that they had come to the same place where Waymouth received a hostile reception. It was the resort of at least a portion of the savages abducted by that explorer, and Skidwarres conducts them directly to the place. Rosier writes of the visit made two years previous: "When we came near the point where we saw their fires" one of the men landed and found "two hundred eighty-three savages, every one his bows and arrows, with their dogs and wolves, which they keep tame at command, and not any thing to exchange at all; but would have drawn us further up into a little narrow nook of a river, for their furs, as they pretended." 3 Mass. Hist. Coll. vol. viii. p 144. That this "little nook of a river" was Pemaquid River appears from the fact that, as Strachey says, Waymouth discovered not only "the most excellent and beneficiall river of Sachadehoc," but that "little one of Pemaquid." The "pond of fresh water, which flowed over the banks" fed "by a strong run," which Rosier says could be made to "drive a mill," is situated on Cape New-aggin, opposite Pemaquid River, and is indicated on one of the maps of the Coast Survey. It has been examined for the writer, and corresponds exactly with Rosier's description, proving that Waymouth had been on the spot. The pond still flows over into the sea.— B. F. D.

marched over a neck of the land * near three miles. So the Skidwarres† brought us to the savages' houses where they did inhabit, although much against his will, for that he told us that they were all removed and gone from the place they were wont to inhabit; but we answered him again that we would not return back until such time as we had spoken with some of them. At length he brought us where they did inhabit, where we found near a hundred of them, men, women, and children, and the chief commander of them is Nahanada.‡ At our first sight of them, upon a howling or cry that they made, they all presently issued forth towards us with their bows and arrows, and we presently made a stand, and suffered them to come near unto us. Then our Indian Skidwarres spoke unto them in their language, showing them what we were, which when Nahanada, their commander, perceived what we were, he caused them all to lay aside their bows and arrows, and came unto us and embraced us, and we did the like to them again.

So we remained with them near two hours and were in their houses.

Then we took our leave of them and returned with our Indian Skidwarres with us towards our ship, the eighth day of August, being Saturday in the afternoon.

Sunday being the 9th of August, in the morning the most part of our whole company of both our ships landed on this island, the which we call St. Georges Island, where the cross standeth, and there we heard a sermon delivered unto us by our preacher,§ giving God thanks for our happy meeting and safe arrival into the country, and so returned aboard again.

Monday being the 10th of August, early in the morning Captain Popham in his shallop with thirty others, and Captain Gilbert in his ship's boat with twenty others accompanied, departed from their ships and sailed towards the river of Pemaquyd, and carried with us the Indian Skidwarres, and came to the river right before their houses, where they no sooner espied us but presently Nahanada with all his Indians with their bows and arrows in their hands came forth upon the sands.

So we caused Skidwarres to speak unto him, and we ourselves spoke unto him in English, giving him to understand our coming tended to no evil towards himself‖ nor any of his people. He told us again he would not that all our people should land. So because we would in no sort offend them, hereupon some ten or twelve of the chief gentlemen ¶ landed, and had some parley together, and afterward they

---

* Pemaquid Point. — B. F. D.

† An Indian who had been carried away by Waymouth in 1605. — B. F. D.

‡ Another of the Indians abducted by Waymouth. — B. F. D.

§ The Rev. Richard Seymour. See Bishop Burgess in the Popham "Memorial Volume," p. 101. Also Bishop Perry's "Connection of the Church of England with Early Discovery and Colonization," Portland, 1863. — B. F. D.

‖ Our copy of the manuscript says "themselffe," but evidently the word intended is *himself*. — B. F. D.

¶ The reader will notice the recurrence of the word "gentlemen," which gives some idea of the reputed *status* of many of the colonists. — B. F. D.

were well contented that all should land. So all landed, we using them with all the kindness that possibly we could; nevertheless, after an hour or two they all suddenly withdrew themselves from us into the woods and left us.

We perceiving this presently embarked ourselves, all except Skidwarres, who was not desirous to return with us.

We seeing this, would in no sort proffer any violence unto him by drawing him perforce, suffered him to remain and stay behind us, he promising to return unto us the next day following, but he held not his promise; so we embarked ourselves, and went unto the other side of the river, and there remained upon the shore the night following.

Tuesday being the 11th of August, we returned and came to our ships where they still remained at anchor under the island we call St. Georges.*

Wednesday being the 12th of August, we weighed our anchor, and set our sails to go for the river of Sagadehock. We kept our course from thence due west until twelve of the clock midnight of the same, then we struck our sails, and laid a hull until the morning, doubting for to overshoot it.

Thursday in the morning, break of the day, being the 13th August, the Island of Sutquin † bore north of us, not past half a league from us, and it riseth in this form hereunder following, the which island lieth right before the mouth of the river Sagadehock south from it near two leagues, but we did not make it to be Sutquin, so we set our sails and stood to the westward for to seek it two leagues further, and not finding the river of Sagadehock, we knew that we had overshot the place; then we would have returned, but could not,‡ and the night in hand. The "Gifte" sent in her shallop and made it, and went into the river this night; but we were constrained to remain at sea all this night, and about midnight there arose a great storm and tempest upon us, the which put us in great danger and hazard of casting away of our ship and our lives, by reason we were so near the shore. The wind blew very hard at south right in upon the shore, so that by no means we could not get off there; we sought all means and did what possible was to be done, for that our lives depended on it. Here we plied it with our ship off and on, all the night, oftentimes espying many sunken rocks and breaches hard by us, enforcing us to put our ship about and stand from them bearing sail when it was more fitter to have taken it in, but that it stood upon our lives to do it, and our boat sunk at our stern, yet would we not cut her from us in hope of the appearing of the day. Thus we continued until the day came; then we perceived ourselves to be hard aboard the lee shore, and no way to escape it but by seeking the shore; then we espied two little islands § lying under our lee.

* Monhegan. — B. F. D.

† Seguin, well known to them through the explorations of Waymouth and Pring. — B. F. D.

‡ Strachey says that it was calm. — B. F. D.

§ The only two islands lying two leagues west of Seguin are Seal Island and the small, nameless rock shown in the Coast Survey Map, No. 5, 1865. Behind the former is safe anchorage, with ten feet at low water. — B. F. D.

So we bore up the helm, and steered in our ship in betwixt them, where, the Lord be praised for it, we found good and safe anchoring. There anchored, the storm still continuing until the next day following.

In this form, being south of it.

Being east and west from the Island of Sutquin, it maketh in this form.*

Friday being the 14th of August, that we anchored under these islands, there we repaired our boat, being very much torn and spoiled; then after we landed on this island,† and found four savages and an old woman; this island is full of pine-trees, of oak, and abundance of whorts of four sorts of them.

Saturday being the 15th of August, the storm ended, and the wind came fair for us to go for Sagadehock, so we weighed our anchors and set sail, and stood to the eastward, and came to the island of Sutquin, which was two leagues from those islands we rode at anchor before, and here we anchored under the Island of Sutquin in the eastern side of it, for that the wind was off the shore that we could not get into the river of Sagadehock, and there Captain Popham's ship's boat came aboard of us, and gave us twenty fresh cods that they had taken, being sent out a-fishing.

Sunday being the 16th of August, Captain Popham sent his shallop unto us for to help us in, so we weighed our anchors, and being calm, we towed in our ship, and came into the river of Sagadehocke, and anchored by the "Gyfte's" side about eleven of the clock the same day.

Monday being the 17th of August, Captain Popham in his shallop with thirty others, and Captain Gilbert in his ship's boat, accompanied with eighteen other persons, departed early in the morning from their ship, and sailed up the river of Sagadehock for to view the river, and also to see where they might find the most convenient place for their plantation, myself being with Captain Gilbert.

So we sailed up into this river near fourteen ‡ leagues, and found it to be a most gallant river, very broad and of a good depth; we never had less water than three fathom when we had zest § and abundance of great fish in it, leaping above the water on each side of us as we sailed.

So the night approaching, after a while we had refreshed ourselves upon the shore, about nine of the clock we set backward to return

---

* The sketches of Seguin are quite fair, especially the first. Champlain named the island "*Tortu*," or the Tortoise, to which it bears a resemblance. In this connection Strachey gives another very rough view of the Union Hills, which is not found in our manuscript. — B. F. D.

† It will be noticed that the language changes to "this island" (Seal Island), as if there were only one island worth mentioning. Strachey errs in saying that the two islands were *west* of Sagadahoc. — B. F. D.

‡ Strachey says incorrectly, "forty." — B. F. D.

§ Our transcriber writes "zest." Strachey made it "sest." Perhaps it should read, "when we had *rest*," or came to anchor. — B. F. D.

and came aboard our ships the next day following, about two of the clock in the afternoon. We find this river to be very pleasant, with many goodly islands in it, to be both large and deep water, having many branches in it: that which we took bendeth itself towards the north-east.*

Tuesday being the 18th, after our return we all went to the shore, and there made choice of a place for our plantation, which is at the very mouth or entry of the river of Sagadehocke on the west side of the river, being almost an island † of a good bigness. Whilst we were upon the shore, there came in three canoes by us, but they would not come near us, but rowed up the river, and so passed away.

Wednesday being the 19th of August, we all went to the shore, where we made choice for our plantation, and there we had a sermon delivered unto us by our preacher, and after the sermon our patent was read with the orders and laws therein prescribed; then we returned aboard our ship again.

Thursday being the 20th of August, all our company landed and there began to fortify. Our president, Captain Popham, set the first spit of ground unto it, and after him all the rest followed, and labored hard in the trenches about it.

Friday, the 21st of August, all hands labored hard about the fort, some in the trench, some for faggots, and our ship carpenters about the building of a small pinnace or shallop.

Saturday, the 22d of August, Captain Popham early in the morning departed in his shallop to go for the river of Pashipakoke.‡ There they had parley with the savages again, who delivered unto them that they had been at wars with Sasanoa, and had slain his son in fight. Skidwarres and Dehanada were in this fight.

Sunday, the 23d, our president, Captain Popham, returned unto us from the river of Pashipscoke.

The 24th all labored about the fort.

Tuesday, the 25th, Captain Gilbert embarked himself and fifteen others with him to go to the westward upon some discovery, but the wind was contrary and forced him back again the same day.

The 26th and 27th all labored hard about the fort.

Friday, the 28th, Captain Gilbert, with fourteen others, myself being one, embarked him to go to the westward again; so the wind serving

---

* They clearly knew the Androscoggin branch, but they ascended the true Kennebec, and must have reached the vicinity of Augusta. — B. F. D.

† The Peninsula of Sabino. Strachey gives the list of officers appointed: "George Popham, gent., was nominated President; Captain Raleigh Gilbert, James Davies, Richard Seymer, Preacher, Captain Richard Davies, Captain Harlow . . . were all sworne assistants." ("Historie of Travaile," p. 172.) Smith says in his "General Historie," "That Honourable patron of virtue, Sir John Popham, Lord Chief Justice of England, . . . sent Captain George Popham for President, Captain Rawleigh Gilbert for Admiral, Edward Harlow, Master of the Ordnance, Captain Robert Davis, Sergeant-Major, Captain Ellis Best, Marshall, Mr. Leaman, Secretary, Captain James Davis to be Captaine of the Fort, Mr. Gome Carew to be searcher: All those were of the council." — B. F. D.

‡ Sheepscot. — B. F. D.

we sailed by many gallant islands, and towards night the wind came contrary against us, so that we were constrained to remain that night under the headland called Semeamis * where we found the land to be most fertile, the trees growing there doth exceed for goodness and length, being the most part of them oak and walnut, growing a great space asunder one from the other, as our parks in England, and no thicket growing under them. Here we also found a gallant place to fortify,† whom nature itself hath already framed, without the hand of man, with a running stream of water hard adjoining under the foot of it.

Saturday, 29th of August, early in the morning we departed from thence, and rowed to the westward, for that the wind was against us; but the wind blew so hard that forced us to remain under an island two leagues from the place we remained the night before. Whilst we remained under this island there passed two canoes by us; after midnight we put from this island in hope to have gotten the place we desired, but the wind arose and blew so hard at south-west contrary for us that forced us to return.

Sunday being the 30th August, returning before the wind we sailed by many goodly islands, for betwixt this headland called Semeamis and the river of Sagadehock, is a great bay in the which lyeth so many islands, and so thick and near together that you cannot well discern to number them, yet may you go in betwixt them in a good ship, for you shall have never less water than eight fathoms. These islands are all overgrown with woods, very thick, as oaks, walnut, pine trees, and many other things growing, as sarsaparilla, hazel-nuts, and whorts in abundance.

So this day we returned to our fort at Sagadehock.

Monday being the last of August, nothing happened; but all labored for the building of the fort, and for the storehouse, to receive our victual.

Tuesday, the 1st of September, there came a canoe unto us in the which was two great kettles of brass; some of our company did parley with them; but they did rest very doubtful of us, and would not suffer more than one at a time to come near unto them, so he departed.

The second day, third and fourth, nothing happened worth the writing, but that each man did his best endeavor for the building of the fort.

Saturday being the 5th of September, there came into the entrance of the river of Sagadehock, nine canoes, in the which was Dehanada and Skidwarres with many others, in the whole near forty persons, men, women, and children; they came and parleyed with us, and we again used them in all friendly manner we could, and gave them victuals for to eat.

So Skidwarres and one more of them stayed with us until night. The rest of them withdrew them in their canoes to the further side of the river; but when night came, for that Skidwarres would needs go to the rest

---

* Cape Elizabeth. — B. F. D.
† On that cape stands Fort Preble. — B. F. D.

of his company. Captain Gilbert, accompanied with James Davis and Captain Ellis Best, took them into our boat and carried them to their company on the further side the river, and there remained amongst them all the night, and early in the morning the savages departed in their canoes for the river of Pemaquid, promising Captain Gilbert to accompany him in their canoes to the river of Penobskott, where the Bashabe remaineth.

The 6th nothing happened; the 7th our ship, the "Mary and John," began to discharge her victuals.

Tuesday being the 8th of September, Captain Gilbert, accompanied with twenty-two others, myself being one of them, departed from the fort to go for the river of Penobskott, taking with him divers sorts of merchandise for to trade with Bashabe, who is the chief commander of those parts; but the wind was contrary against him, so that he could not come to Dahanada and Skidwarres at the time appointed, for it was the eleventh day before he could get to the river of Pemaquid, where they do make their abode.

Friday, the 11th, in the morning early we came into the river of Pemaquid, there to call Nahanada and Skidwarres, as we had promised them, but being there arrived we found no living creature; they all were gone from thence; the which we perceiving, presently departed towards the river of Penobskott, sailing all this day and the 12th and 13th the like, yet by no means could we find it.* So, our victual being spent, we hasten to return. So the wind came fair for us, and we sailed all the fourteenth and fifteenth days, in returning, the wind blowing very hard at north, and this morning, the fifteenth day, we perceived [a] blazing star † in the north-east of us.

The 16th, 17th, 18th, 19th, 20th, 21st, 22d, nothing happened, but all labored hard about the fort and the storehouse for to land our victuals.

The 23d being Wednesday, Captain Gilbert, accompanied with nineteen others, myself one of them, departed from the fort to go for the head of the river of Sagadehock. We sailed all the day; so did we the like the 24th until the evening, then we landed there to remain that night. Here we found champion land and exceeding fertile; so here we remained all night.

The 25th being Friday, early in the morning we departed from hence, and sailed up the river about eight leagues farther, until we came unto an island, being low land and flat. At this island is a great down-fall of water, the which runneth by both sides of this island, very swift and shallow. In this island we found great store of grapes, exceeding good and sweet, of two sorts, both red, but the one of them is a marvellous deep red. By both the sides of this river the grapes grow in abundance, and also very good hops, and also chebolls ‡ and garlic, and for the goodness of the land it doth so far abound that I cannot almost express the same. Here we all went ashore, and with a strong rope made fast to our boat and one man in her to guide her against

---

* If Weymouth or Pring had visited that river in 1605-6, Popham would doubtless have had better directions for finding it. — B. F. D.

† A meteor. — B. F. D.   ‡ A small onion. — B. F. D.

the swift stream, we plucked her up through it perforce. After we had passed this downfall we all went into our boat again, and rowed near a league farther up into the river, and night being at hand, we here stayed all night, and in the first of the night, about ten of the clock, there came on the farther side of the river certain savages, calling unto us in broken English. We answered them again, so for this time they departed.

The 26th being Saturday, there came a canoe unto us, and in there four savages, them that had spoken unto us in the night before. His name that came unto us is Sabenor; he maketh himself unto us to be Lord of the river of Sagadehock.*

[They entertained him friendly, and took him into their boat and presented him with some trifling things, which he accepted; howbeit, he desired some one of our men to be put into his canoe as a pawn for his safety, whereupon Captain Gilbert sent in a man of his, when presently the canoe rowed away from them, with all the speed they could make, up the river. They followed with the shallop, having great care that the Sagamo should not leap overboard. The canoe quickly rowed from them and landed, and the men made to their houses, being near a league in the land from the river's side, and carried our man with them. The shallop, making good way, at length came unto another downfall, which was so shallow and so swift that by no means they could pass any further; for which Captain Gilbert, with nine others, landed and took their fare, the savage Sagamo, with them, and went in search after these other savages, whose houses, the Sagamo told Captain Gilbert, were not far off'; and after a good, tedious march, they came indeed at length unto those savages' houses, where they found near fifty able men, very strong and tall, such as their like before they had not seen, all new painted, and armed with their bows and arrows. Howbeit, after that the Sagamo had talked with them, they delivered back again the man, and used all the rest very friendly, as did ours the like by them, who showed them their commodities of beads, knives, and some copper, of which they seemed very fond, and by way of trade made show that they would come down to the boat, and there bring such things as they had to exchange them for ours. So Captain Gilbert departed from them, and within half an hour after he had gotten to his boat, there came three canoes down unto them, and in them some sixteen savages, and brought with them some tobacco, and certain small skins which were of no value, which Captain Gilbert perceiving, and that they had nothing else wherewith to trade, he caused all his men to come aboard, and, as he would have put from the shore; the savages, perceiving so much, subtly devised how they might put out the fire in the shallop, by which means they saw they should be free from the danger of our men's

---

* What follows, in brackets, is wanting in the Lambeth Library manuscript. It is taken from the Bodleian version of Strachey's work, the number of the manuscript being 1758. The narrative in the Lambeth manuscript ends abruptly at the bottom of the last leaf, as though the following pages had been removed. This portion in brackets corresponds with pages 176-180 in Strachey's printed volume. — B. F. D.

pieces ; and, to perform the same, one of the savages came into the shallop, and taking the firebrand, which one of our company held in his hand thereby to light the matches, as if he would light a pipe of tobacco, as soon as he had gotten it into his hand he presently threw it into the water and leaped out of the shallop. Captain Gilbert, seeing that, suddenly commanded his men to betake them to their muskets, and the targetiers, too, from the head of the boat, and bade one of the men before, with his target on his arm, to step on the shore for more fire : the savages resisted him, and would not suffer him to take any, and some others holding fast the boat rope that the shallop could not put off. Captain Gilbert caused the musketeers to present their pieces, the which the savages seeing, presently let go the boat rope, and betook them to their bows and arrows, and ran into the bushes, nocking their arrows, but did not shoot, neither did ours at them. So the shallop departed from them to the further side of the river, where one of the canoes came unto them, and would have excused the fault of the others. Captain Gilbert made show as if he were still friends, and entertained them kindly, and so left them, returning to the place where he had lodged the night before, and there came to an anchor for that night. The head of the river standeth in 45° and odd minutes.* Upon the continent they found abundance of spruce-trees, such as are able to mast the greatest ship his majesty hath, and many other trees, oak, walnut, pine-apple : fish abundance ; great store of grapes, hops, and chiballs ; also they found certain cods † in which they supposed the cotton wool to grow, and also upon the banks many shells of pearl.

27th. Here they set up a cross and then returned homeward, in the way seeking the by-river of some note called Sasanoa. This day and the next they sought it, when the weather turned foul, and full of fog and rain : they made all haste to the fort, before which, the 29th, they arrived.

30th, and 1st and 2d of October, all busy about the fort.

3d. There came a canoe unto some of the people of the fort, as they were fishing on the sand, in which was Skidwares, who bade them tell their president that Nahanada, with the Bashabae's brother and others, were on the further side of the river, and the next day would come and visit him.

4th. There came two canoes to the fort, in which were Nahanada and his wife, and Skidwares, and the Basshabae's brother, and one other called Amenquin, a Sagamo : all whom the president feasted and entertained with all kindness, both that day and the next, which being Sunday, the president carried them with him to the place of public prayers, which they were at both morning and evening, attending it with great reverence and silence.

6th. The savages departed, all except Amenquin, the Sagamo, who would needs stay amongst our people a long time. Upon the departure of the others, the president gave unto every one of them

---

* This latitude is too high. It was guess-work or a clerical error. — B. F. D.
† An old term for pods. — B. F. D.

copper beads or knives, which contented them not a little, as also delivered a present unto the Basshabae's brother to be presented unto Bassaba, and another for his wife, giving him to understand that he would come unto his court in the river of Penobscot, and see him very shortly, bringing many such like of his country commodities with him.

You may please to understand how,[*] while this business was thus followed here, soon after their first arrival, that had despatched away Captain Robert Davies, in the " Mary and John," to advertise both of their save arrival and forwardness of their plantation within the river of Sachadehoc, with letters to the Lord Chief Justice, importuning a supply for the most necessary wants in the subsisting of a colony to be sent unto them betimes the next year.[†]

After Captain Davies's departure, they fully finished the fort, trenched and fortified it with twelve pieces of ordnance, and built fifty [‡] houses therein, beside a church and storehouse ; and the carpenters framed a pretty pinnace, of about thirty ton, which they called the " Virginia," the chief shipwright being one Digby, of London. Many discoveries, likewise, had been made, both to the main and unto the neighboring rivers, and the frontier nations fully discovered by the diligence of Captain Gilbert. had not the winter proved so extreme unseasonable and frosty ; for it being the year 1607, when the extraordinary frost was felt in most parts of Europe, it was here likewise as vehement, by which no boat could stir upon any business. Howbeit, as time and occasion gave leave, there was nothing omitted which could add unto the benefit or knowledge of the planters, for which, when Captain Davies arrived there in the year following (set out from Topsam, the port town of Exeter, with a ship laden full of victuals, arms, instruments, and tools, &c.), albeit he found Mr. George Popham, the president, and some other dead, yet he found all things in a good forwardness, and many kinds of furs obtained from the Indians by way of trade, good store of sarsaparilla gathered, and the new pinnace all finished. But by reason that Captain Gilbert received letters that his brother was newly dead, and a fair portion of his land fallen unto his share, which required his repair home, and no mines discovered, nor hope thereof, being the main intended benefit expected to uphold the charge of this plantation, and the fear that all the other winters would prove like this first, the company by no means would stay any longer in the country, especially Captain Gilbert being to leave them, and Mr. Popham, as aforesaid, dead ; wherefore they all embarked in this new arrived ship, and in the new pinnace, the " Virginia," and set sail for England. And this was the end of that northern colony upon the River Sachadehoc.]

---

[*] At this point the style of Strachey's narrative changes. The journal of Davies may have been exhausted, or he may have continued it in abstract, or the part which follows may have been drawn from another hand. — B. F. D.

[†] It is nowhere stated that the " Gift " returned in 1607. It is possible, notwithstanding what might be inferred from Strachey, that she remained during the winter. — B. F. D.

[‡] We should undoubtedly read *five*. — B. F. D.

APPENDIX.

The original sources of information concerning the Sagadahoc Colony, which were known previous to the publication of the Strachey volume in 1849, by the Hakluyt Society, were, — 1. Sir Ferdinando Gorges's "Brief Narration," written not long before his death, in 1647, and left in manuscript, and not published till 1658. The narrative is strangely wanting, in many parts of it, in dates; and many of the dates which are introduced are erroneous. Some of its errors are probably due to a lack of memory, others to a faulty press. Notwithstanding all these defects, the book is indispensable, and many of its errors may be corrected by other writings. Only a small part of the tract relates to the Sagadahoc Colony. 2. The "Brief Relation" of the President and Council for New England, published in 1622. The Council for New England was substantially a reincorporation of the first or Northern Colony of Virginia; and inherited its traditions, and entered into its labors. 3. Smith's "Generall Historie," pp. 203, 204, published in 1624. This book has some details taken from original sources. 4. Purchas's "Pilgrimage," 1614. In the margin, at p. 756, and repeated in the later editions of 1617 and 1626, are some detached facts about the colony, which the compiler selected from the letters or journals of the colonists, and from the notes of Hakluyt, whose papers came into Purchas's possession. From all these sources combined, the account afforded of the Sagadahoc settlement is of the most meagre character. We fail to get more than a glimpse of the life of the colony during the severe winter they experienced there, and of the circumstances attending the return of more than half the colonists in December, and of the final breaking up and return of the remainder, when the ship or "ships" came back with supplies the next year. Besides, we were sadly deficient in data for the greater part of the events. Neither did the Strachey narrative, published thirty years ago, supply these desiderata, as regards the concluding part of the colonists' history, nor, indeed, does that we now publish, which is substantially the basis or Strachey's account. We shall yet have to wait patiently for the letters or journals of other colonists, namely, John Eliot, George Popham, Raleigh Gilbert, and Edward Harlow, seen by Purchas, to come to light.

We now extract for publication, as an appendix to the foregoing narrative of the Sagadahoc Colony, the several accounts named above, in order that the reader may have before him all the original sources of information that our early chronicles afford. In the editorial Preface, we have already made several extracts from these accounts. We also append a brief extract from Sir William Alexander's "Encouragement to Colonies."

B. F. D.

From Sir Ferdinando Gorges's " Brief Narration." London, 1658, *pp.* 8-10.

" The Despatch of the First Plantation, for the Second Colony sent from Plymouth."

" By the same authority all things fully agreed upon between both the Colonies, the Lord Chief Justice [Popham], his friends and associates of the West Country, sent from Plymouth Captain Popham as president for that employment, with Captain Rawley Gilbert and divers other gentlemen of note in three sail of ships * with one hundred landmen, for the seizing such a place as they were directed unto by the Council of that colony, who departed from the coast of England the one and thirtieth day of May, A. D. 1607, and arrived at their rendezvous the 8th of August following; as soon as the president had taken notice of the place, and given order for landing the provisions, he despatched away Captain Gilbert, with Skitwarres his guide, for the thorough discovery of the rivers and habitations of the natives, by whom he was brought to several of them, where he found civil entertainment, and kind respects, far from brutish or savage natures, so as they suddenly became familiar friends, especially by the means of Dehamda and Skitwarrers, who had been in England; Dehamda being sent by the Lord Chief Justice with Captain Prin, and Skitwarres by me in company, so as the president was earnestly entreated by Sassenow, Aberemet, and others the principal Sagamores (as they call their great lords), to go to the Bashabas, who, it seems, was their king, and held a state agreeable, expecting that all strangers should have their address to him, not he to them.

" To whom the president would have gone after several invitations, but was hindered by cross winds and foul weather, so as he was forced to return back, without making good what he had promised, much to the grief of those Sagamores that were to attend him. The Bashabas notwithstanding, hearing of his misfortune, sent his own son to visit him, and to beat a trade with him for furs. How it succeeded, I could not understand, for that the ships were to be despatched away for England, the winter being already come; for it was the fifteenth day of December before they set sail to return, who brought with them the success of what had past in that employment, which so soon as it came to the Lord Chief Justice's hands, he gave out order to the council for sending them back with supplies necessary.†

" The supplies being furnished and all things ready only attending for a fair wind, which happened not before the news of the Chief Justice's death was posted to them to be transported to the discomfort of the poor planters; but the ships arriving there in good time was a

---

* Strachey, and our narrative, which he used, and the " Brief Relation," say *two ships.* — B. F. D.

† Sir Ferdinando's memory is here at fault. Chief Justice Popham had died as early as the 7th June, 1607, a week only after the expedition sailed for Sagadahoc. His son, Sir Francis Popham, interested himself in sending the supplies. Strachey speaks of but one ship being despatched for England, the " Mary and John." — B. F. D.

great refreshing to those that had had their storehouse and most of their provisions burnt the winter before.

"Besides that, they were strangely perplexed with the great and unseasonable cold they suffered with that extremity, as the like hath not been heard of since, and it seems was universal, it being the same year that our Thames was so locked up that they built their boats upon it, and sold provisions of several sorts to those that delighted in the novelties of the times. But the miseries they had past were nothing to that they suffered by the disastrous news they received of the death of the Lord Chief Justice, that suddenly followed the death of their president; but the latter was not so strange, in that he was well stricken in years before he went, and had long been an infirm man. Howsoever heartened by hopes, willing he was to die in acting something that might be serviceable to God, and honorable to his country, but that of the death of the Chief Justice was such a corrosive to all as struck them with despair of future remedy, and it was the more augmented, when they heard of the [death of] Sir John Gilbert, elder brother of Ralph Gilbert * that was then their president, a man worthy to be beloved of them all for his industry and care for their well being. The president was to return to settle the estate his brother had left him, upon which all resolved to quit the place, and with one consent to [come] away, by which means all our former hopes were frozen to death, though Sir Francis Popham could not so give it over, but continued to send thither several years after in hope of better fortunes, but found it fruitless, and was necessitated at last to sit down with the loss he had already undergone.

"Although I was interested in all those misfortunes, and found it wholly given over by the body of the adventurers, as well for that they had lost the principal support of the design, as also that the country itself was branded by the return of the plantation, as being over-cold, and in respect of that, not habitable by our nation.

"Besides, they understood it to be a task too great for particular persons to undertake, though the country itself, the rivers, havens, harbors, upon that coast might in time prove profitable to us.

"These last acknowledgments bound me confidently to prosecute my first resolution, not doubting but God would effect that which man despaired of, as for those reasons, the causes of others' discouragements, the first only was given to me, in that I had lost so noble a friend, and my nation so worthy a subject. As for the coldness of the clime, I had had too much experience in the world to be frightened with such a blast, as knowing many great kingdoms and large territories more northerly seated, and by many degrees colder than the clime from whence they came, yet plentifully inhabited, and divers of them stored with no better commodities from trade and commerce than those parts afforded, if like industry, art, and labor be used, for the last I had no reason greatly to despair of means when God should be pleased, by our ordinary frequenting that country, to make it appear, it would

---

* Rawley Gilbert. — B. F. D.

yield both profit and content to as many as aimed thereat, these being truly, for the most part, the motives that all men labor, howsoever otherwise adjoined, with fair colors and goodly shadows.'

From *"A Brief Relation of the Discovery and Plantation of New England." London, 1622, pp. 2–4.*

"Hereupon Captain Popham, Captain Rawley Gilbert, and others were sent away with two ships and an hundred landmen, ordnance, and other provisions necessary for their sustentation and defence, until other supply might be sent. In the mean while, before they could return, it pleased God to take from us this worthy member, the Lord Chief Justice, whose sudden death did so astonish the hearts of the most part of the adventurers, as some grew cold, and some did wholly abandon the business. Yet Sir Francis Popham, his son, certain of his private friends, and other of us, omitted not the next year, holding on our first resolution, to join in sending forth a new supply, which was accordingly performed.

"But the ships arriving there did not only bring uncomfortable news of the death of the Lord Chief Justice, together with the death of Sir John Gilbert, the elder brother unto Captain Rawley Gilbert, who at that time was president of that council, but found that the old Captain Popham was also dead; who was the only man, indeed, that died there that winter, wherein they endured the greater extremities; for that in the depth thereof, their lodgings and stores were burnt, and they thereby wondrously distressed.

"This calamity and evil news, together with the resolution that Captain Gilbert was forced to take for his own return (in that he was to succeed his brother in the inheritance of his lands in England), made the whole company to resolve upon nothing but their return with the ships; and for that present to leave the country again, having in the time of their abode there (notwithstanding the coldness of the season, and the small help they had), built a pretty bark of their own, which served them to good purpose, as easing them in their returning.

"The arrival of these people here in England was a wonderful discouragement to all the first undertakers, insomuch as there was no more speech of settling any other plantation in those parts for a long time after; only Sir Francis Popham having the ships and provision which remained of the company, and supplying what was necessary for his purpose, sent divers times to the coasts for trade and fishing; of whose loss or gains himself is best able to give account.

---

* After relating the sending out of Captain Henry Challons, whose voyage was " overthrown "; and the despatch of Captain Thomas Hanam, to " second " Challons, who could not be found; and that the Lord Chief Justice Popham, and his associates, on Hanam's favorable report of the country, " waxed so confident of the business, that the year following every man of any worth, formerly interested in it, was willing to join in the charge for sending over a competent number of people to lay the ground of a hopeful plantation," the narrative proceeds as above. — B. F. D.

" Our people abandoning the plantation in this sort as you have heard, the Frenchmen immediately took the opportunity to settle themselves within our limits." *

From Captain John Smith's "Generall Historie of New England," fol. London, 1624. pp. 203, 204.

" Concerning this History you are to understand the letters-patents granted by his Majesty in 1606, for the limitation of Virginia, did extend from 34° to 44°, which was divided in two parts : namely, the first colony and the second. The first was to the honorable city of London, and such as would adventure with them to discover and take their choice where they would, betwixt the degrees of 34 and 41. The second was appropriated to the cities of Bristol, Exeter, and Plimoth, &c., and the west parts of England, and all those that would adventure and join with them, and they might make their choice anywhere betwixt the degrees of 38 and 44, provided there should be at least one hundred miles distance betwixt these two colonies, each of which had laws, privileges, and authority for the government, and advancing their several plantations alike. Now this part of America hath formerly been called Norumbega, Virginia, Nuskoncus, Penaquida, Cannada, and such other names as those that ranged the coast pleased. But because it was so mountainous, rocky, and full of isles, few have adventured much to trouble it, but as is formerly related : notwithstanding, that honorable patron of virtue, Sir John Popham, Lord Chief Justice of England, in the year 1606, procured means and men to possess it, and sent Captain George Popham for President : Captain Rawley Gilbert for Admiral ; Captain Edward Harlow, Master of the Ordnance ; Captain Robert Davis, Sergeant-Major ; Captain Elis Best, Marshal ; Master Seaman, Secretary ; Captain James Davis to be Captain of the Fort ; Master Gome Carew, Chief Searcher. All those were of the Council, who, with some hundred more, were to stay in the country. They set sail from Plimouth the last of May, and fell with Monahigan the 11th of August. At Sagadahock, nine or ten leagues southward, they planted themselves at the mouth of a fair, navigable river, but the coast all thereabouts most extreme stony and rocky ; that extreme frozen winter was so cold they could not range nor search the country, and their provision so small, they were glad to send all but forty-five of their company back again. Their noble president, Captain Popham, died, and not long after arrived two ships well provided of all necessaries to supply them, and some small time after another,† by whom under-

---

* The narrative then proceeds to speak of Argall's expedition, in which he proceeded " to displace" the Frenchmen who had built forts at " Mount Mansell, Saint Croix, and Port Reall." — B. F. D.

† Strachey, p. 179, speaks of but one ship returning to the colony with supplies, that commanded by Captain (Robert) Davies, adding, that in this ship and the new pinnace, the " Virginia," the colony " all embarked" for England. — B. F. D.

standing of the death of the Lord Chief Justice, and also of Sir John
Gilbert, whose lands there the president, Rawley Gilbert, was to
possess, according to the adventurer's directions, finding nothing but
extreme extremities, they all returned for England in the year 1608,
and thus this plantation was begun and ended in one year, and the
country esteemed as a cold, barren, mountainous, rocky desert."

From Purchas's " Pilgrimage." London, 1614, *p.* 756.*

" A. D. 1607, was settled a plantation in the River Sagadahoc; the
ships called the " Gift " and the " Mary and John,† being sent thither by
that famous English Justicer, Sir John Popham, and others. They found
this coast of Virginia full of islands, but safe. They chose the place of
their plantation at the mouth of Sagadahoc, in a westerly peninsula:
there heard a sermon, read their patent and laws, and built a fort.
They sailed up to discover the river and country, and encountered
with an island where was a great fall of water, over which they hauled
their boat with a rope, and came to another fall, shallow, swift, and
unpassable. They found the country stored with grapes, white and
red, good hops, onions, garlic, oaks, walnuts, the soil good. The head
of the river is in forty-five and odd minutes. Cape Sinicamis in 43°
30', a good place to fortify. Their fort bare name of Saint George.
Forty-five remained there,‡ Captain George Popham being President,
Raleigh Gilbert, Admiral. The people seemed affected with our men's
devotions, and would say King James is a good king, his God a good
God, and Tanto naught. So they call an evil spirit which haunts them
every moon, and makes them worship him for fear. He commanded
them not to dwell near or come among the English, threatening to
kill some and inflict sickness on others, beginning with two of their
Sagamos children, saying he had power, and would do the like to the
English the next moon, to wit, in December.

" The people§ told our men of cannibals, near Sagadahoc, with
teeth three inches long, but they saw them not. In the river of
Tamescot they found oysters nine inches in length; and were told that
on the other side there were twice as great. On the 18th of January
they had, in seven hours' space, thunder, lightning, rain, frost, snow,
all in abundance, the last continuing. On February 5 the president
died. The savages remove their dwellings in winter nearest the deer.
They have a kind of shoes a yard long, fourteen inches broad, made
like a racket, with strong twine or sinews of a deer; in the midst is a
hole wherein they put their foot, buckling it fast. When a Sagamos
dieth they black themselves, and at the same time yearly renew their
mourning with great howling; as they then did for Kashurakeny, who

* In the margin of the book from which this account is taken, Purchas
places his authorities. We have therefore placed these names at foot, leading
from the words in the text as they are given in Purchas. — B. F. D.
† James Davies.
‡ Jo. Eliot. G. Pop. Let. to S. I. Gilbert and E. S.
§ Ral. Gilbert.

die l the year before. They report that the cannibals have a sea behind them. They found a bath two miles about, so hot that they could not drink it. Mr. Patteson was slain by the savages of Nanhoc, a river of the Tarentines. Their short commons* caused fear of mutiny. One of the savages, called Aminquin, for a straw hat and knife given him, stripped himself of his clothing of beaver's skins, worth in England fifty shillings or three pounds, to present them to the president, leaving only a flap to cover his privities. He would also have come with them for England. In winter they are poor † and weak, and do not then company with their wives, but in summer when they are fat and lusty. But your eyes wearied with this Northern view, which in that winter communicated with us in extremity of cold, look now for greater hopes in the Southern Plantation, as the right arm of this Virginian body, with greater costs and numbers furnished from hence."‡

From Sir William Alexander's " Encouragement to Colonies," &c. London, 1624, p. 30. §

"That which is now called New England was first comprehended within the patent of Virginia. being the north-east part thereof. It was undertaken in a patent by a company of gentlemen in the west of England, one of whom was Sir John Popham, then chief justice, who sent the first company that went of purpose to inhabit there near to Sagadahoc ; but those that went thither, being pressed to that enterprise, as endangered by the law, or by their own necessities (no enforced thing proving pleasant, discontented persons suffering, while as they act can seldom have good success and never satisfaction), they after a winter stay, dreaming to themselves of new hopes at home, returned back with the first occasion, and to justify the suddenness of their return, they did coin many excuses, burdening the bounds where they had been with all the aspersions that possibly could devise, seeking by that means to discourage all others, whose provident forwardness importuning a good success, might make their base sluggishness for abandoning the beginning of a good work to be the more condemned."

* Edward Hurley.
† Other notes ap. Hak.
‡ This extract was first published in this, the second edition, of the " Pilgrimage "; also in the third edition, 1617, and in the fourth, 1626. A copy of this last edition usually accompanies the four volumes of Purchas's " Pilgrims," London, 1625, another work, and is commonly cited as vol. v. of that book.— B. F. D.
§ In printing this extract from Sir William Alexander, we would remark, that the phrase " endangered by the law," might refer to poor debtors, and does not necessarily imply that the Sagadahoc colonists, or any part of them, were criminals. We have seen no evidence that they bore that character, and no laws existed at that time authorizing the transportation of criminals to Virginia. — B. F. D.

www.ingramcontent.com/pod-product-compliance
Lightning Source LLC
Chambersburg PA
CBHW021600270326
41931CB00009B/1305